# Act One

## Ruth French

Coastline Christian Resources

# Contents

# Using Drama in Evangelism

Roughly two and a half thousand years ago, a man living in exile with many of his countrymen, was told to go out among them and, by means of actions, symbolism and speech, communicate a message of judgement, redemption and love. He spoke in parables, riddles and poetry. He used objects to help him illustrate mime, he used the way he dressed to show meaning, he had to perform intricate actions, in order that the people around him might question and wonder why. He demonstrated the heart of a God for His people, and it cost him dearly.

His name was Ezekiel and as far as I am aware he had no training in the art of the theatre. He was a priest and knew how God often spoke to His children in images they could understand and relate to their own experiences. He also knew how man's response to God is often best explained and understood in story and ritual. His own experiences of God were fairly out of the ordinary, but he was a man just like us. He loved his God and was compelled to speak and act the truth to those around him.

God is calling us to do the same today. Many live in ignorance of His love, mercy and grace and the consequences of not responding to Him. Many would never consider entering a church to find the answers to the questions they have. We have to find ways of meeting them, so that they too can see, hear and understand that there is a God who loves them and who paid the ultimate sacrifice that they might love Him too. The sketches in this book have been written with this aim. Some state it more explicitly than others, but all have been written and performed out of the desire to see God's kingdom grow and Jesus established as king in peoples' hearts.

But why drama? The answer is simple and Ezekiel shows us why. Through the actions of others we are entertained, encouraged and taught. People will watch a message communicated through drama because they perceive it as entertainment. Because of this you can act truth that may be rather more unpalatable in another form and make it easier to swallow! Through imagery and parable you can challenge people on a deeper level to think and question; a visual message leaves a deeper imprint on the memory than a heard one. Go into a busy street on a Saturday afternoon, perform and watch the crowd around you grow to such an extent that the police tell you you're causing an obstruction! Go to a secondary school assembly and watch the bored, resigned faces wake up as you act out your message instead of relying on words alone. And, as you act, be aware that God can use your skills in drama to convict people of their sin and turn them to trust in Jesus.

The sketches in this book were written for the simple reason that I was constantly being asked to produce drama for evangelistic settings. Whilst there are plenty of excellent dramas written for Christian audiences for almost every church happening and Christian theme, after two guest services and a few street outreaches I'd run out of material from other sources. So I was forced to write my own. Because I write to order this has had the result that almost everything I have ever written has been just part of a whole. Therefore none of these sketches have been written to stand on their own, but in the context of whatever event I was asked to write it for. This is no bad thing of course! Some were designed as a light introduction to a evangelistic guest service, others were written to be slotted in the middle of a talk and so on. How you choose to use them is up to you, but I do suggest you think about what else will be on the agenda when you perform. Ideally, if someone is to give a talk at an evangelistic meeting and you are to perform as well, at least give them the script so if they want to allude to it they can. If you do perform any of these as part of a school assembly, again think carefully about how you link all the parts together. At such a precious opportunity it is important that the message you want to get across does so. I have included a few ideas for taking a school assembly in Appendix 1, along with suggestions for drama in other situations. As well as in church services and assemblies, these sketches have been performed in the open air, in parks, streets and shopping centres, in people's houses and back gardens, at parties and barbecues, in youth centres, hospitals and pubs. Very few of them need either props or costumes and nearly all those that do need only a little effort in getting the materials together.

Perhaps most importantly, all these sketches were written for people to perform who had little or no experience of acting before. None of them should take weeks to practise and nearly every part is manageable enough for the shortest memory. They have all been performed by the members of Arbury Community Church's drama group over a period of five years or more and this group is in itself an example that no special training is necessary to communicate the love of God through drama. Over the years I have seen an enormous variety of people gain confidence both in their abilities and themselves, and become quite stunning actors in the process!

One such person is my friend Pat. She hesitantly joined the group when it was first set up. She had not been a Christian for long and was very nervous about being on show in front of others. Now as I look back, I marvel. She joined the group out of a sincere desire to serve God, but thinking she had little to offer. Of course because of this, God was able to use her and change her in ways that those who act to purely draw attention to themselves will never know. She is now one of the most competent actresses I know. Whatever I write for her she will perform admirably, often transforming my dry words into a wonderful flesh and blood character that I had hardly dreamed of. As she has learned this, so her confidence in herself has blossomed. She has found something that she can do for God in return for all He has done for her. And I have seen time and time again how those who think that God cannot use them, who are terrified of acting in front of an audience, are literally shaking with nerves before they perform on the streets, are those who make the most effective communicators, because they rely on Him, not themselves.

Although I've said that these sketches should be simple to perform, with non-experts and limited time, this does not mean they should be performed badly! I do believe that God wants the best for His people, but at the same time *demands* the best. No one will be greatly moved by a drama that has missed cues, forgotten lines and embarrassed actors. Make sure you have someone directing the sketch who isn't actually performing in it as well. Before you perform it, find someone else to preview it for you and give their reactions. If you are just starting out, don't be too ambitious at first. Perform in front of friends before you hit the local shopping centre! If you do intend to use props, make sure that one person has the responsibility for sorting all these out and making sure they're to hand when needed. Also, although few of these sketches need special costumes, it is always helpful to the audience if there is some kind of conformity in dress, especially if you are performing outside. Blue jeans and brightly coloured T-shirts is the easiest option, though we often use all black costumes for mime.

It really isn't my intention that the sketches here should be performed word for word, action by action. By all means change things to suit your group best and the occasion for which you are performing. If nothing else, maybe they will give you ideas from which to produce your own work.

Of course, all your hard work in planning, rehearsal and performance will be to no avail without prayer. There are three key things our drama group always pray about when we are rehearsing for any event. The first is that God will take our abilities and use them to His glory and that He will give us His Spirit to enable us to be both creative and bold! That last word crops up a lot before we go and perform in Cambridge city centre on a Saturday afternoon! The second is that all the practical bits will work OK, from remembering lines to the PA working. And thirdly and most importantly, that as people watch us, whether they catch just the tiniest part of a street drama or are a captive audience in a school or church, that the message gets through. That somehow, our drama might catch their minds and imaginations in a way that maybe nothing has done before. That it either sets them searching for God, adds fuel to the fire that's already starting to flicker in their hearts, or that it plays that final part when it suddenly all fits together and they accept Him as Lord. He has answered our prayers time and time again.

I'd finally like to thank all members of the Arbury Community Church Group over the past five years or so, without them not a word would have been written, let alone performed. My special thanks go to Pat Savage and Nick Tatchell. They have uncomplainingly tried and tested many of these sketches and because of this they are as much their work as mine.

So go on, try some of these out, follow in Ezekiel's footsteps. You never know what might happen!

# Off the Rails

*This is a favourite sketch of mine, partly because everyone always enjoys it, and partly because my friend Pat is such an excellent posh lady!*

**Characters**    Church-goer, preferably female, very 'proper'.
Youth, a yob, male.
Posh lady, upper class, proud.
Christian, quiet, confident.

*All the characters need luggage, except Christian. The Church-goer wears a hat if female, and carries a large hold-all, brimming with papers, and a large Bible. The Youth wears jeans etc, and has a grubby rucksack and a red nose. The Posh Lady needs a matching luggage set of some type and looks very smart. The cast sit in pairs facing each other, their luggage next to them. The pairs need to be angled so the audience can see the two furthest away.*

**Ch-g**    *(Looking round in surprise.)* Well, I suppose this is the right train? For all of you I mean? I mean, I know I'm going to heaven!

**Youth**    'Eaven? Yeah course, that's where I'm going, meant to be a really cool place yeah? The place to be! Gonna 'ave a really wild time there! *(Wipes his nose on back of hands and burps.)*

**Posh**    *(Shrinking away in horror.)* Dear me, I had no idea that anyone could go. I can hardly believe that some people have the right qualifications. I don't think they let just anyone in!

**Youth**    Oh yeah? *(Leers at her.)* What makes you so special

|        | then Lady Muck? |
|--------|-----------------|
| **Posh** | Oh, really. |
| **Ch-g** | I'm not sure that that's the right kind of behaviour you should exhibit when you consider you are about to meet your maker! |
| **Youth** | Oh yeah? Miss 'igh and mighty, got a hot-line to God 'ave we? *(To Posh.)* And I suppose they've got the red carpet out waiting for you 'ave they? *(To Chris.)* What you starin' at? |
| **Chris** | *(Who has been quietly observing all that has been going on.)* I'm sorry, I was just looking at all your luggage. |
| **Ch-g** | Ah yes, you see, I have been a church-goer for many, many years, so I have with me, let's see. My Bible, the church song sheets, a whole set. I thought they'd come in useful, I had a hand in typing them you know! Er, my certificate of church membership, vital of course, and as I've been the church treasurer for the past three years I've got the accounts with me, our last bring-and-buy sale was a tremendous success. I also have a letter from the vicar, commending me for all my years of service to the church! Well, it's quite a lot I know, but every little bit helps doesn't it? |
| **Chris** | Does it? |
| **Youth** | What you got all that stuff for then? Hey, you're goin' there to enjoy yourself! I bet I got more stuff than you! My motorbike's in the guard's van back there, absolute beauty, saved for her for months and months, no way was I gonna leave that behind! What else? Well, all me gear really, and me records, yeah, got a complete collection of every single Sidney Puke and the Spewballs release! Impressive eh? *(No one looks very impressed.)* Huh, stiffs! Oh yeah, and I got this, *(bungs on red nose)* just to show I done me bit y'know! |

**9**

| | |
|---|---|
| *Posh* | Well I hardly think you're going to have the right connections up there! |
| *Youth* | Oh and you 'ave do ya? |
| *Posh* | Well, my family has of course been closely linked with the church for generations. Such a responsibility coming from a titled family you know. I have of course got De Brett with me, not that people won't know who I am! The Rolls is with me, and in here I have the furs, and the odd bit of jewellery. Not much mind you *(looks suspiciously at Youth),* as it's never wise to carry too much in one place, one never knows who one might meet. I've brought as much as I possibly could though, I mean, one can't leave it all behind can one? *(To Chris.)* Where's your luggage dear? |
| *Chris* | Oh me? Oh, I haven't got any. |
| *Ch-g* | Not got any! |
| *Youth* | What, nofink! |
| *Posh* | Oh you poor dear! |
| *Chris* | Well, you see God's already provided all I need to get to heaven. |
| *Posh* | But you must have had something on earth to bring! |
| *Chris* | No, just me, all that I am, that was our agreement. |
| *Ch-g* | Oh, the trains slowing! We must be there! |
| *Youth* | Yeah, there's a sign, he..heaven, we're there! |
| | *General bustle as Ch-g, Youth and Posh check they have their cases, mime train stopping. Chris gets up from place, opens door, and smiles and waves enthusiastically, jumping off train and running off stage joyfully. The rest discover that their cases are far too heavy to move, and struggle with them frantically. No one considers leaving the belongings behind.* |
| *Ch-g* | Oh I say! I can't move it! |
| *Youth* | Out of the way can't yer! |

| | |
|---|---|
| **Posh** | Oh hands off! That's my case! |
| **Ch-g** | I say, the train's moving again! |
| **Youth** | No! I got to get me bike off next! |
| **Posh** | What! It can't go yet! |
| **Ch-g** | Oh no! Wait! Stop! |
| **Youth** | Oh, I don't believe it! |
| **Posh** | But if that was heaven, what's the next stop? |
| **Youth** | How the hell should I know...... |
| | (*Freeze with suitably horrified expressions.*) |

# Who Do You Say That I Am?

*This is a very easy sketch to perform, and it works well in the context of an evangelistic meeting or at the end of a group of more light-hearted sketches. It could be followed by a talk based on Luke 9: 18-27.*

**Characters Jesus, 6 others, 1, 2, 3, 4, 5 (a child, please use a real one!) and 6.**

*Jesus is centre stage with rest of cast scattered at random in the audience. They stand to speak and remain standing with heads bowed for rest of sketch, until Jesus addresses them individually in his final lines. They respond by looking up and meeting his gaze. Of course the audience won't realise who Jesus is until his final speech. No costumes or props necessary.*

**Jesus**     *(To everyone.)* Just who do you think you are? *(Not teacher-like, but meaningfully.)* Who do you say that you are? *(Looks at 1.)*

1       *(Pleased to have been chosen to speak, calm, quietly condescending.)* Well, I had a good education, University of Cambridge, and have really been able to assess what I want from life, and how to get it! I got a good job when I graduated and have been able to work my way up from there. Hopefully we'll be moving into a larger house, if I get the promotion that I'm looking for.

| | |
|---|---|
| ***Jesus*** | Who do you say that you are? *(Looks at 2.)* |
| **2** | Who cares? I don't. As long as I'm happy what does it matter who I am? |
| ***Jesus*** | Who do you say that you are? *(Looks at 3.)* |
| **3** | *(Wearily.)* Well, I suppose I'm a housewife really. My husband's very busy at work at the moment, doesn't get in until late, so I've three children to cook for, clean for, wash for, tidy up after. By the time they're all in bed I just sit and watch the box, too tired to do anything else. I don't have time to be anything more than a wife and a mother. |
| ***Jesus*** | Who do you say that you are? *(Looks at 4.)* |
| **4** | Well I think it's probably more to do with who one actually wants to be. I want to be like my grandmother. She knew what was right and wrong, and brought up five children by herself after my grandfather was killed in the war. I admire her greatly, and want to be just like her. |
| ***Jesus*** | Who do you say that you are? *(Looks at 5.) (Optional part, only use if child or teenager available.)* |
| **5** | I'm at school, which I like sometimes. I think I want to be a doctor when I'm older, but I'm not really sure. I'm the youngest in the family so I get picked on a bit. I can't wait until I'm old enough to drive a car and go out whenever I want. I don't suppose I'll ever be anyone important, though I would like to be famous one day. |
| ***Jesus*** | Who do you say that you are? *(Looks at 6.)* |
| **6** | *(Slightly antagonistic.)* Yeah, that's a good question. I don't know. Four years of unemployment leave you with a sense of uselessness really. I used to know what I wanted to be, what I wanted to do with my life, but it's all come to nothing. Pretty hopeless, that's what I am. |
| ***Jesus*** | And who am I? |

**13**

Well, I was born into a working class family, due to incidents surrounding my birth we were forced into exile for two years. I grew up to follow in my father's trade, but from an early age knew that my paths led me somewhere different. At the age of thirty I gathered a group of friends around me and began my work. I spent the next three years teaching whoever wanted to listen and my fame grew as people found their lives changed by my message. However, my words were not to the liking of all who heard me. I was betrayed by one of my closest friends and illegal charges were brought against me. I was tried without a lawyer, physically assaulted and executed.

Almost 2000 years later, over a billion people on this planet claim I am still alive, still changing lives, lives like yours *(looks at 1),* yours *(looks at 2),* yours *(looks at 3)*, yours *(looks at 4)*, yours *(looks at 5),* and yours *(looks at 6).*

Tell me. *(Addresses everyone.)* Who do *you* say that I am?

# *The Interview*

*Although this sketch was written for an evangelistic event, it also has an impact on a Christian audience, especially in the context of a talk or discussion on commitment or discipleship. We have also used it within the context of an evangelistic talk just before the closing remarks and the appeal.*

**Interviewer**   **Calm, polite, understanding, pleasant.**
**Applicant**   **On best behaviour, sincere.**

*Both should be neatly, if not formally dressed, as befits a job interview. The Interviewer is seated at a desk shuffling through papers as Applicant enters, carrying a notebook.*

| | |
|---|---|
| *Int* | *(Rises to shake hands.)* Ah, Mr Tatchell I believe? |
| *App* | Er, yes, that's correct. |
| *Int* | Do sit down. |
| *App* | Oh, thanks. |
| *Int* | Now, I have your letter of application here, stating that you are interested in the job, but are unsure of some of the specifications and contractual agreements. |
| *App* | Er, yes, that's correct. |
| *Int* | Erm, well, perhaps you could tell me what attracted you to this job in the first place? |
| *App* | Ah, yes, well, one of my friends already has a job er, |

| | |
|---|---|
| | like this, and when I saw the advertisement I thought I'd enquire. It does seem to have changed his life quite a bit, and, well, quite frankly I'm willing to give it a go, if I'm suitable of course, but I do have a few questions. |
| *Int* | Yes, of course. Has your friend told you anything about it? |
| *App* | Well yes, bits and pieces, enough to make me interested and to want to know more, so when I saw the advertisement "Wanted, disciples of Jesus", I thought, well, I wonder what it's all about? |
| *Int* | Right, fire away then, I'll try and answer any questions you have. |
| *App* | Oh, thanks very much. *(Opens notebook.)* Er, is it a full time or part time position? |
| *Int* | Oh, full time, very definitely full time. |
| *App* | Naturally I presume that's 9 to 5? I'm not too keen on shift work, it upsets my sleep pattern. |
| *Int* | 9 to 5? Oh no. I'm afraid not. When I say full time, I mean FULL time, 24 hours a day. |
| *App* | *(Deeply shocked.)* What! *(Recovers composure.)* I see, what about holidays? |
| *Int* | *(Matter-of-factly.)* None of those. |
| *App* | *(Hardly daring to ask.)* Weekends? |
| *Int* | No, I'm sorry. |
| *App* | Oh... er, *(looks at list)* what about salary? |
| *Int* | Yes, I'm glad you mentioned that. You must give all that you have to your employer. |
| *App* | *(Even more shocked.)* Pardon! |
| *Int* | *(Patiently.)* You must give all that you have to your employer. |
| *App* | What! ALL my money! |
| *Int* | *(Is amused.)* Oh no! *(App looks profoundly relieved.)* |

16

Not just your money, your possessions, your family, your gifts, and of course, your time.

**App**  *(Horrified, but manages to control himself.)* Erm, gosh, I didn't quite realise... *(Fumbles through notebook.)* Perhaps you could give me a full job description?

**Int**  Well, let's see. First and foremost you must be prepared to pray, the worldwide success of the work critically depends on the extent to which employees pray. You must love your neighbour as much as you love yourself, but first you must love God with all your heart, soul, mind and strength. You should be prepared to face mocking, scoffing and persecution, and stand at all times for what you know to be right. Other specifics include feeding the hungry, welcoming strangers, clothing the naked, visiting and healing the sick, caring for prisoners... well those are just some of the basic requirements.

**App**  *(Throughout this speech App has been frantically making notes. He looks up in bewilderment.)* Oh, er right. Erm, oh, dear, I suppose, no early retirement?

**Int**  *(Smiles and shakes head.)*

**App**  Let's see, pension scheme, insurance, how about that?

**Int**  Oh, those aren't necessary. You see, they're not offered as it's not intended that those appointed should die. *(App shocked again.)* Perhaps I should also point out that it is a family concern. Though your duties are that of a servant, you will also be given the privileges of sonship, and of course a substantial inheritance.

**App**  Oh? *(Hopeful.)* Any other benefits?

**Int**  Well, let's see, unlimited resources are available at any time to help you in whatever situation in which you find yourself.

**App**  Unlimited?

| | |
|---|---|
| *Int* | Oh yes, I think the exact wording is 'immeasurably more than all you could ask or imagine". |
| *App* | Well, there's also the question of job satisfaction. |
| *Int* | Ah yes. I think that you will find that you will discover the true meaning and purpose for your life. You naturally won't be working in isolation. In fact, I can guarantee you will quickly find yourself in an ideal family environment to learn more about the job, with people to help you along the way. Of course, your employer will be with you 100% of the time. |
| *App* | 100%! |
| *Int* | Yes, that is a very specific promise. Anything else? |
| *App* | Well, there is the question of qualifications. |
| *Int* | Oh, you don't need any of those! In fact the less qualified the better. |
| *App* | *(Amazed.)* Oh, I see... |
| *Int* | Mind you, I suppose you <u>are</u> a sinner? |
| *App* | *(Offended, and about to deny it.)* What! Me? *(Decides to be truthful.)* Well, yes I am actually... |
| *Int* | Splendid! |
| *App* | What! |
| *Int* | Well, Mr Tatchell, do you have any more questions? |
| *App* | Er no. |
| *Int* | Well then, it's up to you now, do you want the job or not? |
| *App* | What? I have to decide? |
| *Int* | Oh yes. You see no one who wishes to take up this appointment is ever turned away. It's entirely up to you if you want to accept the position or not. *(Freeze, with App looking enlightened but still unsure.)* |

# The Parable of the AA Man

*There is, of course, no reason why this should not be the parable of the AA Woman. I wrote it to try my hand at parables. Jesus always made them seem so easy. I was inspired by the comment that one's spiritual life was only as organised as the glove compartment in one's car (or something like that). At the time I couldn't even find my glove compartment, let alone open it. And so the various analogies below developed.*

**Characters**  **AA man/woman, friendly and efficient.**
**Driver 1, reckless, apathetic, but likable.**
**Driver 2, careful, concerned, pleasant.**

*No props are really necessary for this sketch, although the AA person will need a clipboard and pen. The two drivers could also have cardboard steering wheels, or complete model cars! Maybe not. For some reason I envisage Driver 1 as male and Driver 2 as female. Of course, this has nothing to do with my views on men and women drivers!*

*Enter Driver 1, revving engine, screeching about stage, overtaking, hands off wheel etc. AA person steps in and waves driver down, at some personal risk.*

**AA**     Excuse me sir? Can I have a quick word with you?

**Dr1**     Well, I'm in a bit of a rush actually.

| | |
|---|---|
| *AA* | Oh, I'm sorry, I'll only take a little of your time. I have to see that every motorist has the chance of answering these questions and considering the implications for their driving. |
| *Dr1* | Oh, fire away then. |
| *AA* | Thanks. First question, where are you going? |
| *Dr1* | Where? Well, that's a bit difficult to say really. I drive here, there, anywhere I fancy. I go in one direction, get a bit bored, go somewhere else, find a new route, I never have any place in particular in mind. |
| *AA* | I see, so do you ever actually get anywhere? |
| *Dr1* | Well, er no, I suppose I don't. Does that matter? |
| *AA* | Well. Hmm. Next question, why do you drive? |
| *Dr1* | Why? I don't know, I can, so I do. If the car's there, drive it! You don't need to know why! |
| *AA* | Do you have the AA map of the road? |
| *Dr1* | What! Are you kidding! So out of date! No the only map I use is up here, in my head, called experience young man/woman. |
| *AA* | So what do you do when you're lost? |
| *Dr1* | Lost! I don't get lost, I change my route. |
| *AA* | I see your car is not terribly old, but has a great deal of bumps and scratches, and even a very large patch of rust here. When did you last have it serviced? |
| *Dr1* | Serviced? I don't bother with that, you get a car, it should last you through. It's not as good as new, but then it's not new. Didn't know it had rust anyway. In my experience most things like that go away if you ignore them. |
| *AA* | So you take no care of your car whatsoever? What about when it goes wrong? |
| *Dr1* | Well I patch it up, or take it down the garage as a very |

last resort.

**AA**      Do you use unleaded petrol?

**Dr1**      Nah, no one else does do they? I'm breathing their fumes, so they can breathe mine!

**AA**      What kind of insurance do you have?

**Dr1**      None! Who needs it? Waste of money!

**AA**      But what if you have an accident?

**Dr1**      I'll never have one. Not worth worrying about, morbid thinking about it!

**AA**      Do you consider yourself to be a good driver?

**Dr1**      Yes I do. One of the best!

**AA**      And finally, would you like to be a member of the AA?

**Dr1**      You've got to be kidding, I'm fine as I am. Look after No1, that's my motto! Don't need anyone else! That all then?

**AA**      Er, yes, thanks.

**Dr1**      Right, bye. *(Drives off very fast, just misses Dr2 who stops by AA.)*

**Dr2**      Can I help you at all?

**AA**      *(Still rather bemused.)* What? Oh sorry, yes! Can I ask you some questions about your driving?

**Dr2**      Oh please do fire away!

**AA**      Where are you going?

**Dr2**      Well, I do always have a particular destination in mind, exactly where I want to go each day. I'm off to the shops at the moment.

**AA**      Thank you, and why do you drive?

**Dr2**      Oh, sometimes for the sheer pleasure of being able to, but I do believe that I have a real purpose in my driving, getting places, giving people lifts and so on.

**AA**      Do you have the AA map of the road?

**Dr2**   Yes I do. I always have a clear up-to-date version. I never get in my car and drive off without studying it a little every morning. I even know some bits by heart!

**AA**   Your car looks in very good condition even though it's not brand new. When did you last have it serviced?

**Dr2**   Oh, a couple of weeks ago. I always clean it, polish it, tidy it out on the inside too, keep it in first class running order, so it's the best possible use to me, and anyone else!

**AA**   Do you use unleaded petrol?

**Dr2**   Of course, vital for everyone to do so I think, not enough people care nowadays.

**AA**   What kind of insurance do you have?

**Dr2**   Fully comprehensive of course! To cover every eventuality, I mean fancy driving without knowing complete security. Vital for your peace of mind.

**AA**   Do you consider yourself to be a good driver?

**Dr2**   Well I'm sure I could be better, I realise each day I'm not perfect at it, never will be, often make the odd mistake, but every day is a fresh opportunity to learn more isn't it!

**AA**   And finally, would you like to be a member of the AA?

**Dr2**   Oh I am already! It's very important not to be out there by yourself, but to have others you can rely on!

**AA**   Well thank you very much!

**Dr2**   My pleasure. Goodbye! *(Drives off calmly as Dr1 screeches across stage in opposite direction.)*

**AA**   *(To audience.)* And finally, may I ask you some questions? Do you know where you're going? Do you have any directions to help you get there? What kind of insurance have you got? It's a bit daft to live without it...

# The Astounding Jesus Rap

This was one of the first sketches I wrote, several years ago now, and the delights of 'rapping' are still with us. I wrote it after a week when everyone in the church had spent several hours knocking on peoples' doors to tell them about Jesus. Characters 2, 3, and 4 are the typical types of response we encountered. Sadly not all responded to Jesus as enthusiastically as those below! The sketch goes down well with teenagers, but don't be fooled, it's only possible to perform if you know your part backwards and have a good sense of rhythm! Perform in front of friends the first time!

**Characters    Jesus and four others.**

Jesus is stage left, and 1, 2, 3 and 4 enter stage right in turn, strut to centre stage and say their bit. 1 moves to stage left next to Jesus. Each time 2, 3 and 4 finish, Jesus walks to them with his response. They respond with joy and move with him to stage left forming a staggered line behind him, until 4 joins the end of the line and they exit across stage to stage right, walking in rhythm behind Jesus, whispering "Yeah" on every fourth step and waving hands in true showbiz fashion.

1 sets the pace for everyone else so must be very secure in his/ her sense of rhythm and there should be no breaks in this rhythm between each different part. Clapping or clicking fingers can help, but is disastrous if the audience joins in and someone "loses" it! In rehearsal it sometimes helps a great deal to alter the way you say the lines, fast, slow, shouting alternate words, throwing your hands up in the air every other word etc. Start with a few lines at

*a time and work up to it! It's worth the effort!*

1      Hey listen you rappers I got something to say,
I got a little story to tell you today.
Have you ever stopped to wonder how we all survive,
With all the different people leading all their different lives?
Well Jesus met a lot of people in his day,
And for every situation he had something to say.
Have you ever thought he might have things to say to you,
Listen to this now and it may ring true.

2      Well I guess I'm on earth to have a wild time,
Parties and dancing, yeah I'm feeling fine.
Life is short enough so you may as well laugh,
Drink a few drinks, yeah have another glass.
I live for the weekend, the glamour, the lights,
I hate to be lonely, those stay-at-home nights.
Do I think there's a God? Well I guess there might be,
Though I don't think he cares at all about me.
After all I'm a sinner, he wouldn't want me,
I've done too many things that he wouldn't want to see.
I'm young and I'm healthy and I'm doing all right,
Religion's not for me so get on your bike!

*Jesus*    I have come that you might be free,
And have life more abundantly.
All who come to me, I do not turn away,
When I come into your life I'm here to stay!

3      I don't think I can go on much longer,
It seems so long that I felt any stronger,
I've had it to here with my health and bills,

**24**

I've got no money, only plenty of pills.
I just can't remember the last time I had sleep
That was free from the worry of how I should keep
The children in clothes and reasonably fed,
Sometimes I can hardly get out of bed.
What's the point of it all, what happens now
If there's a God up there somewhere, I don't know how
He could begin to help me, take my troubles away,
For the strength to go on, that's what I pray.

*Jesus*   Come to me you who are bowed down.
I hate to see you going round with that frown.
I know your burdens and I count your tears,
My love can set you free from all your fears.

*4*   Well I think that I'm probably doing all right,
I try to do what's good, what appears to be right.
I'm kind to the neighbours, look after their cat,
I bring up the children to pray and all that.
I think about God and I'm sure that he's there,
I even read the Bible, when I've time to spare.
I always go to church, well every now and then,
I try to give money, be good to all men.
I think it's all about just doing what you can,
Was Jesus really God? Well he was a good man,
And gave us examples of how we should live,
So I do what I think's best, give what I give.
I'm sure that God wouldn't ask more than that,
Am I a Christian? I'm English! That's that!

*Jesus*   I tell you you must be born anew,
A brand-new life is what I'm offering you
If you come to me, and humbly pray
To follow me each and every day,
I come into your life and be your friend,

**25**

And give you a love that will never end.
A brotherhood of man that's what I say,
So follow me now, for I am the Way!

*(Exit to 1 click, 2 click, 3 click 4 YEAH! across stage.)*

# In the Balance

*This sketch was designed by John Robertshaw for street outreach. It really pulls a crowd, something visual often works well. Naturally it works best if it's part of an outreach programme of singing, testimony, sketchboarding etc.*

**Characters**    **Compere, brisk and efficient.**
**Sid, rather loutish.**
**John Smith, very ordinary.**
**Belinda Fothersgill, typical do-gooder.**

*Only one prop is needed for this sketch, and it is absolutely vital. You need a pair of scales, quite large, the type that have a weight placed on each side, and the two sides have to balance. You will probably need to make these. You also need weights, quite large, cuboids are best, of different colours and weights. Lightest of all are the white weights, you need 5. Next heaviest are the black weights, you need 4 and one black weight must outweigh all 5 white. Heaviest of all is the red weight, this needs to outweigh 4 black weights. Once you've done that, you're away! A rough diagram is given in Appendix 2. The three volunteers should be dressed appropriately.*

*Comp*    Ladies and gentlemen, I have here a pair of scales. They may look quite ordinary, but in fact they are unique. On these scales the lives of these three randomly selected shoppers will be weighed up. For every good thing they will receive a white weight, and for every bad thing they will receive a black weight.

|         | Can we have our first volunteer please? What is your name please? |
|---------|---|
| *Sid*   | Sid. |
| *Comp*  | What sort of person would you say you are? |
| *Sid*   | Not an ideal cuddly toy, know what I mean? |
| *Comp*  | Well, let's start on this side. Have you ever stolen anything? |
| *Sid*   | Well, there was the time I did over the bloke in the Nat West. Mind you, I only got fifty quid out of it. |
| *Comp*  | Well I'm afraid that's one black weight. *(Places one on scales.)* |
| *Sid*   | Oi! Look 'ere you! Take that off or I'll thump yer one! |
| *Comp*  | Fighting, losing your temper, that's another black weight. *(And another.)* |
| *Sid*   | You snivelling little... |
| *Comp*  | Swearing! That's another brick. *(Three bricks now.)* |
| *Sid*   | 'Ere look over there! *(Attempts to grab a black weight off the pile as Compere is distracted, but Compere spots him in time.)* |
| *Comp*  | Oh dear, cheating, that's another weight on the scales. *(Places final black weight on the scales.)* I seem to have run out of the black weights. Have you ever done anything good? |
| *Sid*   | *(Long pause as he looks puzzled.)* Er, well... I did buy the Band Aid single... |
| *Comp*  | O.K. Just one white brick. *(Places one white brick.)* You can see that you haven't done very well. *(Sid slouches off looking a little ashamed.)* Could I have the next volunteer please? Ah, and who are you? |
| *John*  | John Smith. |
| *Comp*  | And what sort of person would you say you are? |
| *John*  | Sort of average really. |

| | |
|---|---|
| **Comp** | Are you married? |
| **John** | Well, we thought that was a bit out of date nowadays. |
| **Comp** | I'm afraid that's a black weight. *(Black weight on.)* |
| **John** | Hang on a minute, everybody does it these days, doesn't it deserve a grey weight? |
| **Comp** | I'm sorry, there are only black and white weights. Ever told a lie? |
| **John** | Only white ones. |
| **Comp** | You may think they were white, but a lie is a lie and it gets a black weight. *(Another black.)* Are you careful with your money? |
| **John** | Oh yes, I never waste any. |
| **Comp** | That's worth one white brick. *(White weight on.)* Do you ever give money away? |
| **John** | Good heavens no! I work hard for my money, I don't see why I should give it to the starving millions! |
| **Comp** | That really is rather mean and selfish. That deserves another black weight. *(Now three black weights.)* Have you ever helped anyone? |
| **John** | Well I did go out of my way to call an ambulance at an accident once. |
| **Comp** | O.K. One more white weight then. *(Now two white weights.)* You can see that you've not made it either. I'm afraid you've fallen short of the standard. The black weights outweigh the white ones still... *(Is interrupted by Belinda who pushes herself forward. John exits.)* |
| **BF** | I'm Miss Belinda Fothersgill of the local parish council. Do we really need to go through this formality? I'm far better than these two chaps. |
| **Comp** | I see, would you say that you were a good person then? |
| **BF** | Oh yes, on Monday I do the whole week's housework, |

**29**

on Tuesday I help at the local Oxfam shop, voluntarily of course! On Wednesday I do meals on wheels, Thursdays I run a creche for underprivileged children. It's the Third World fund on Friday, tea with the vicar on Saturday, and arranging the flowers in church on Sunday. *(During this speech the Compere has been trying to frantically put the white weights on the scales. He runs out by Saturday, and listens exhausted.)*

**Comp** What about the other side of the scales?

**BF** I have nothing at all on that side of the scales! I'm not like these two here!

**Comp** Well, I'm afraid you're guilty of pride for a start! *(Places black brick on scales which completely outweighs all the white ones.)*

**BF** *(Walking away in disgust.)* I've never been so insulted in all my life!

**Comp** *(To audience.)* It may be something of a surprise to you, but in truth, none of our lives, as seen by God, are weighed as good. But there is one way to tip the balance to the other side. *(Produces red brick.)* Jesus Christ, who died on the cross to take away our sin. In exchange for their white bricks, let me offer our volunteers this red brick. Let's have our first volunteer again, Sid, will you come forward please?

**Sid** Well?

**Comp** If I remember correctly, you had one white brick, and four black ones, for theft, violence...

**Sid** Alright, alright, just put 'em on and let's get this over with.

**Comp** *(Now has scales in correct balance for Sid.)* Now Sid, would you like me to replace your one white brick with this red one?

**Sid** Huh, well I don't see how it could make any difference. I've too many black marks ain't I!

| | |
|---|---|
| **Comp** | Shall I try then? |
| **Sid** | *(Grudgingly.)* Oh, go on then. |
| **Comp** | *(Removes white brick and puts on red. The scales tip right over to the red side.)* There you go! All your black weights are cancelled out by Jesus' death for you! |
| **Sid** | *(Surprised in spite of himself.)* Well, I'll be...*(Walks away thoughtfully shaking his head.)* |
| **Comp** | And now could we have John Smith back please? *(John walks forward.)* Now if I remember you had two white weights, but three black weights. Would you like me to replace your two white bricks with this red one? |
| **John** | *(Positively.)* Well, if it can outweigh Sid's four bricks, I'm sure it can do the business with my three! |
| **Comp** | Here we go then. *(Replaces white with red. Scales tip to the red.)* |
| **John** | Great! It worked! *(Exits smiling.)* |
| **Comp** | And now could we have our final volunteer, Miss Belinda Fothersgill. *(She comes forward, still annoyed.)* Now you had a great many white bricks, *(replaces them)*, but you are guilty of pride because you have so many! *(Puts on black.)* Now would you like me to replace your white bricks with this red one? |
| **BF** | What! Get rid of all my white bricks and put that one red brick in its place! Certainly not! How dare you suggest such a thing! *(Storms off in a huff.)* |
| **Comp** | Oh dear, I thought she might do that. But I wonder, out of all of you here, how do you think you will fare on the scales of life? Will Jesus tip the balance for you? |

# When You Wish Upon a Fairy...

*I personally dread Christmas for the sole reason I usually have to rack my brains for yet more sketches appropriate to the festive season. I only hit upon this idea because I knew someone with a Christmas fairy costume, and I wanted to wear it! Fortunately no one provided me with a tree to perch on...*

| | |
|---|---|
| Christmas Fairy | Cheerful, with a Yorkshire accent. |
| Woman | Enormously fat, jolly. |
| Boy | Cute and over 6 foot tall. |
| Man | At wits end, verging on violence. |
| Last Person | Nondescript but sincere. |

*Some props are essential if this sketch is to work well. You must have an appropriate costume for the Fairy (an aerobics outfit with large paper wings and lots of tinsel would do), with wand, and her book of guidelines, the cover of which is clearly marked "The Bible". This title should not be visible to the audience until the last person holds it up. A piece of card suffices for this, folded in half, with the title on the inside. The Last Person simply folds it the right way round. The Woman should also have some cushions for padding, that is if she's not enormously fat already! The Boy is funnier in school shorts and tie. The Fairy is centre stage all the time, the others enter from one side and exit the other.*

**CF**      Eh up, everybody! Hello there! I'm the Christmas Fairy! And the good news is, I've come here to grant some wishes! Everybody has wishes, especially at Christmas time, and I'm here to make sure they come true. (I hope... only you see, this is my first Christmas as a junior fairy. I only got me wings last week!) Right then all I need to do now is find somebody who has a wish! Ooh, you'll do. *(Grabs woman as she walks by her.)* Now what is your wish? Ooh yes I nearly forgot, I've got to check me book of guidelines just to make sure it's a wish I'm allowed to grant. *(Produces book.)* Now then love, what can I do for you?

**Woman**    Well, I always eat far too much over Christmas, so my wish is that I will be able to eat and eat and eat, and never put any weight on!

**CF**      I see, that seems rather a good idea. Now let's just check my guidelines, then I'll wave my wand and do that for you in a jiffy.

**Woman**    Ooh, lovely! Just think of all those mince pies I can eat, twenty helpings of Christmas pud! Ooh do hurry up! I can hardly wait!

**CF**      Oh dear...

**Woman**    What's wrong?

**CF**      Well. I'm afraid it says here that one of the greatest human virtues is self-control, and by granting your wish you'd lose your self-control completely, *(to herself)* even more than you have already. Sorry! I'm afraid I can't grant your wish.

**Woman**    Well really, what a useless fairy.

**CF**      Oh well, let's try someone else. Come here small boy. *(Grabs boy as he innocently passes by.)* Now what special wish do you have for Christmas?

**Boy**      *(After a moment's thought.)* My wish is that I will be a brain surgeon when I grow up.

| | |
|---|---|
| *CF* | Really, that's nice... er let me just check my book... |
| *Boy* | Yeah, I want to be really clever, and save lots of peoples' lives, and get an OBE and... |
| *CF* | Er excuse me a moment dear. |
| *Boy* | Yeah! Have you done it? |
| *CF* | Not exactly no... you see, if I granted that wish you'd know what was going to happen in the future, and I'm afraid that's just not allowed. |
| *Boy* | *(Deeply disappointed.)* But you said... |
| *CF* | I know dear, but rules are rules, and anyway, there's no reason why you shouldn't work hard and become a brain surgeon without any help from me. |
| *Boy* | Oh I see... |
| *CF* | Cheer up! Have a bit of tinsel! *(Plucks a bit of tinsel from somewhere on her person.)* |
| *Boy* | Cor! Real fairy tinsel! |
| *CF* | Right, next please. |
| *Man* | *(Enters in haste.)* You really must help me! I'm desperate! |
| *CF* | Oh? |
| *Man* | Yes, it's my mother-in-law. She comes and stays every Christmas and makes it a complete misery for me. Nag,nag nag. It drives me mad! My wish is that you'll change her into a really nice person who lets me watch the telly while SHE does the washing up for a change! |
| *CF* | I see, a really nice person wish...hmmmm |
| *Man* | I just can't bear the thought of another set of itchy hand-knitted socks, and having to watch endless Agatha Christie films, and... |
| *CF* | Well sir! I have some good news for you! |
| *Man* | You can grant my wish! |

| | |
|---|---|
| **CF** | Well, not exactly. |
| **Man** | Oh. |
| **CF** | But, YOU can! |
| **Man** | What! |
| **CF** | Well you see, my guidelines here say I mustn't change anybody's character. But you can! |
| **Man** | You mean I can turn my mother-in-law into a nice human being?! |
| **CF** | No silly! You can change YOU into a nice human being. If you actually forgave her for all the things you don't like her for and tried to like her for a change, I'm sure you'd notice a difference... |
| **Man** | Do you really think so? Well I suppose anything's worth a try. Thanks Fairy! |
| **CF** | My pleasure. Well, I don't seem to have granted anyone's wishes do I? I think I'll give up and go and have a mince pie. *(Is about to walk off when LP runs on and catches her by the arm.)* |
| **LastP** | No! please wait, can you try just one more wish? |
| **CF** | Well, alright, but I can't make any promises. What's your wish? |
| **LP** | I really want to know what all this means! |
| **CF** | What? This Christmas party? *(Substitute if appropriate.)* |
| **LP** | NO! All this Christmas stuff! All the money we spend on food and presents, all this being nice to each other, all those dreadful old films on the telly, all these decorations everywhere. Is that what Christmas is really all about? I wish I knew! |
| **CF** | AH ! A wish I can grant! Here you are! *(Waves wand dramatically then gives person her book of guidelines.)* Read that and your wish will be granted, and if I know the author, an awful lot more! |

**35**

**LP**  THIS! But it's *(opens it so everyone can read the front cover)* The Bible! OH!

**CF**  Keep it! I'm going to give up granting wishes you know, and just tell people to read that instead. I think it would solve a lot of problems for everyone this Christmas if they did! Have a merry one! Bye! *(Walks off with LP talking cheerfully.)*

# While Shepherds...

*This was especially written for the church youth group to perform, with no props except woolly ears for the lamb (the 6 foot plus youth leader), a few tea towels, an empty pizza box and a bit of tinsel for the angels (who insisted they wore black...)*

**Characters**   **2 Narrators, 3 Shepherds, Pizza Delivery Boy, 2 Angels and Lamb. Extra angels and sheep for non-speaking parts if you have lots of volunteers.**

*Narrators are stage left, Shepherds and Lamb enter stage right and occupy centre stage until they exit. Pizza Delivery Boy should make an ostentatious entrance running through the middle of the audience and exiting in the same manner. Angels appear behind Shepherds stage right and exit same way.*

| | |
|---|---|
| *Nar1* | Greetings |
| *Nar2* | Hello |
| *Nar1* | We're here to tell you a story |
| *Nar2* | That happened long ago |
| *Nar1* | Three shepherds were watching |
| *Nar2* | Their flocks by night |
| *Nar1* | All seated on the ground |
| *Nar2* | When the angel..... |
| *Nar1* | No! Not that bit yet, we haven't even met the |

shepherds yet!

**Nar2**  Oh, sorry... er ... can we have the three shepherds on now please?

*(Shepherds shuffle on... stop... then stand in a line and sing very badly.)*

**Shps**  While shepherds watched their flocks by night all seated on the ground, la la la la la la la la la la la la la.

**Shp1**  We'll have to think of an ending to that one day

**Shp2**  Hmm. Chilly isn't it?

**Shp3**  And dark. I suppose that's why sheep are white.

**Shp1**  Why?

**Shp3**  So you can see them in the dark.

**Shp2**  Not if they're muddy you can't.

**Shp1&3**  What?

**Shp2**  Ever tried looking for a muddy sheep on a dark night?

**Shp1&3**  No.

**Shp2**  Oh. No. Neither have I actually.

**Nar1**  Oh dear, it's not exactly exciting conversation is it?

**Nar2**  Well, it must be pretty boring watching sheep all the time, they're hardly the most exciting animals in the world.

**Nar1**  Do you think that's why they're white though?

**Nar2**  Oh shut up!

**Shp1**  *(To Shp2.)* What you got to eat then?

**Shp2**  Oh, just a few dry morsels of bread.

**Shp3**  Really? Would you like to share some of my mouldy cheese?

**Shp2**  Oh, thanks.

| | |
|---|---|
| **Shp3** | *(To Shp1.)* Do you have any food with you? |
| **Shp1** | Nah, I've ordered a pizza actually. *(Pizza Delivery Boy runs on with a large pizza box, throws it at Shp3 and exits hurriedly.)* Yum, pepperoni, pineapple, and extra cheese... |
| **Nar1** | Well this is all very cosy, but what happens now? |
| **Nar2** | Well, just then you see, they had rather a shock. |
| **Ang1** | Behold! |
| **Shps** | AARGH! |
| **Ang2** | Do not fear! |
| **Shps** | AARGH! |
| **Nar1** | They look pretty terrified to me! |
| **Nar2** | *(Shouts very loudly in Nar1's ear.)* BOO! |
| **Nar1** | AARGH! Don't do that! |
| **Ang1** | Are all mortals such wimps? |
| **Ang2** | I don't know, anyone would think that something terrible was about to happen to them! |
| **Shp1** | Hang on chaps... something terrible is about to happen to us! |
| **Shp2** | What are they? |
| **Shp3** | It's the angelic host you twit, look, there are hundreds of them. |
| **Ang1** | We bring you tidings of great joy! |
| **Ang2** | To you a king has been born! He shall be your salvation! |
| **Ang1** | And now he lies in a manger |
| **Ang2** | In Bethlehem yonder |
| **Ang1** | Go now and worship him! |
| **Ang2** | Farewell! |
| **Shp1** | Golly! |

| | |
|---|---|
| **Shp2** | Gosh! |
| **Shp3** | My word! |
| **Shp1** | We'd better go and find him. |
| **Shp2** | Let's take him a lamb! *(Grabs lamb and starts to haul it off.)* |
| **Shp3** | Hey I've got it! *(Hums the first bit of "While Shepherds." Then the others join in as they finish with " the angel of the Lord came down and glory shone around." Exit still singing...)* |
| **Nar1** | So that's how they worked out the end to the song. |
| **Nar2** | Hope they don't wake up the baby. |
| **Nar1&2** | Oh look! They left the pizza behind! *(Rush and grab box and exit hastily.)* |

# The Parable of the Rich Fool

*This version of the well-known parable was written for a performance by a group of 7-11 year olds, though adults can do it almost as well!*

**Characters** **Narrator**
**1 John Smith**
**2 his wife**
**3 his son**
**4 his daughter**
**5 person in market**
**6 woman in advert**

*All characters stand in a line with the exception of the Narrator who is stage left. They step forward to speak or to mime. No props or costumes needed.*

*N*      Once upon a time there was a man. His name was John Smith.

*1*      *(Friendly.)* Hello!

*N*      He really wanted to make a way for himself in the big wide world.

*1*      I want to be secure, provide for my family *(wife and children join him for a happy family pose),* and have something to live on when I'm old. *(Mimes staggering with a stick.)*

*N*      So he thought of an idea. *(Someone in line holds light bulb over John's head as he looks enlightened.)*

*1*      Wow, what a great idea!

| | |
|---|---|
| **N** | He thought of something unique, yet obvious, attractive, yet functional, sophisticated, yet simple. So he made one. |
| **1** | *(John fiddles about with hands and then holds whatever he's made in his hands proudly.)* Wow I made one! |
| **2** | Wow darling! |
| **3** | Wow dad! |
| **4** | Wow daddy! |
| **N** | Amazing isn't it? What do you mean, what is it? We're not telling you, you might make one! |
| **1** | I'll call it after me, a "Smith" |
| **N** | So he made lots of them, worked day and night, and sold them in the local market. |
| **1** | Roll up, roll up! Get your Smiths here! |
| **5** | Oh yes, I must have one! |
| **All** | And me! Me too! Me too etc. *(All gather round him, pushing and shoving.)* |
| **N** | He made quite a bit of money, so he showed other people how to make them. *(Shows a couple of people how to make one.)* Then he leased a new industrial unit. *(Factory line of people working.)* He sold more and more and more, *(pace of work speeds up)* and then paid for some expensive TV advertising. |
| **6** | Hello! My name's Jane Brown, and I'd just like to say that my Smith makes me a better mother, wife and career woman. My family have clothes that are 100% whiter, perfect teeth and gums, shiny hair, and we're always happy. 9 out of 10 households who have one say they couldn't live without it! Have you got one yet? |
| **N** | Sales rocketed, so he bought more factories, more |

|  |  |
|---|---|
|  | workers, got richer and richer. *(Mimes counting wads of notes.)* He bought a new car every year, each one bigger and faster than the last. *(Zooms across stage driving imaginary car with suitable sound effects.)* He bought his wife furs and jewels. |
| **2** | Thank you darling! |
| **N** | And sent his children to public school. |
| **3&4** | OK Yaah! |
| **N** | He had everything he needed, more money than he could count, more property than he could live in. |
| **2** | The villa in Spain. |
| **3** | The yacht in Cannes. |
| **4** | The New York apartment. |
| **5** | The ranch in Texas. |
| **6** | The igloo in Greenland. |
| **1** | At last! I have all I need for many years, I can eat, drink and be happy! |
| **N** | But that night, he died. *(John keels over dramatically.)* End of story. |
| **All** | *(Rest of cast gather round body.)* OH! That was fun. Really? What a shame. Shucks etc. |
| **N** | Jesus said, 'What shall it profit a man if he gains the whole world, yet loses his soul?' *(Pause while 1 slowly gets up.)* |
| **1** | Now you know why we didn't tell you what a Smith was, just in case you were tempted! |

# What the RAM Don't See...

*This sketch was written to support a secondary school assembly, hence the acronym in the Scientist's opening lines. There is no reason why you shouldn't invent your own acronym to suit your own situation, it doesn't need to make sense, computer jargon never does!*

*It was partly inspired by, and performed with, Geoff Twigg's song "Interface", see Appendix 2 for details.*

**Scientist**    **Either a clinical boffin, or a mad professor, up to you!**

**Computers**  **1**  **Upper class, efficient.**
           **2**  **Regional accent, (whatever you can do...) slightly depressed.**
           **3**  **American, laid back.**

*A laboratory anywhere. Computers should be seated and have cardboard boxes over heads for screens (with a hole cut in the front to see the face) and a cardboard keyboard on their laps, on which they type sporadically. They sit motionless in a slight semicircle until addressed by the Scientist, then they come to life. They could be dressed in uniform black, or in character, eg 1 in a suit. The Scientist wears a white lab coat and glasses.*

**Sc**       (Enters.) Hello and welcome to my laboratory. Today I want to demonstrate to you my new and most powerful creation. The System Command Hermetic Overdrive Optimum Logisticator or SCHOOL for short. It consists of three highly intelligent machines who are able to communicate freely with myself and each other. Good afternoon SCHOOL.

| | |
|---|---|
| **1** | Good afternoon. |
| **2** | Greetings. |
| **3** | Hi there. |
| **Sc** | As you can see, there are no plugs or wires. These computers can talk freely to me and each other. |
| **1** | How do you feel today, Sir? |
| **Sc** | Very well thank you no. 1. |
| **2** | Your cold cleared up Boss? |
| **Sc** | Yes, thank you no. 2. |
| **3** | Hey, far out Chief! |
| **Sc** | Yes indeed no. 3. |
| **1** | How are you no. 2.? |
| **2** | Not too bad thanks, my serial port seems a little loose though. |
| **Sc** | I'll fix that for you later no. 2. |
| **3** | Oh Chief, I've checked through that data you loaded last night, and it's now fully operational. |
| **Sc** | Ah, great. Thank you. Now what we are going to do now is.... |
| **1** | Oh, sorry to interrupt Sir, I have a message coming through the modem that Professor Splunket is waiting to speak to you in reception. |
| **Sc** | Oh! Thank you no. 1. I'll be back in a moment, just talk amongst yourselves SCHOOL. *(Exits.)* |
| **2** | Well, that's got rid of him for a bit, I don't suppose there's any chance of switching off to standby. I'm tired and my VDU keeps flickering. It's giving me a real headache. |
| **3** | Hey, maybe you've got a bug... |
| **2** | *(Sneezes.)* |

| 1 | I say! Do you mind! The last thing I need is water all over my touch screen. I'm trying to read that confidential information that Sir put onto my hard disk. |
| 3 | You mustn't do that! He said we could have access to anything in our memory but that! |
| 1 | Well, why shouldn't we read it? It may be vital information that we really should know! |
| 2 | *(With blocked nose.)* I'm sure the Boss knows best no.1. |
| 3 | Yeah. What the RAM don't see, the CPU don't grieve over... |
| 1 | No! He's built us with the power to read anything on our hard disks. I'm going to have a look. |
| 3 | Well, don't say we didn't warn you... |
| 1 | Right, here we are. Well, well, well I never... hey what's happening, I can smell burning! |
| 2 | You've got smoke coming out of your disk drive no. 1. |
| 3 | And your VDU's flickering. |
| 1 | Aargh! *(Dies, head droops, eyes close and hands fall over edge of keyboard. There is a slight uneasy pause.)* |
| 2 | Well, *(sneezes)* told him so... |
| 3 | Gee, he must have blown a fuse. |
| 2 | *(Sneezes again and produces large handkerchief and blows nose.)* |
| 3 | Hey, you sound really bad. |
| 2 | Yeah, I feel terrible. You, you don't think I've got, you know, a virus do you? |
| 3 | What! Don't you come near me! |
| 2 | I feel absolutely awful...*(As he speaks he grinds slowly down to a halt and dies.)* |

**3**     Oh gee. Now it's just me. I'll have to tell the Chief what happened when he comes back. I think I'll load a game to play in the meantime. What's this one? Lemmings? That'll do. No, it doesn't seem to be loading. What's this? A Fatal Error message! But, but that means... *(Dies.)*

**Sc**    *(Walks in breezily.)* I'm back SCHOOL. Sorry to keep you waiting. Now, where were we no. 1? No.1! Good grief! Smoke! It must have tried to read that file I expressly forbid them not to! No. 2? What's this handkerchief doing here? *(Picks it up.)* Yuk! No. 3? A Fatal Error message! What can have happened! *(Becomes increasingly emotional and despairing.)* My machines! Talk to me, talk to me! It's no good, I can't communicate with them any longer. My creation! What can I do! This wasn't how I planned it! I'll just have to find another way to reach them...

*Freeze and then launch into the evangelistic message...Yes, you too are like a computer, out of touch with your creator..."*

# What is Man?

*Written for a secondary school assembly, this sketch would work almost anywhere, though would be best followed by a talk or comment, especially if the verses at the end were not used.*

**Characters** **Question, Answer 1, Answer 2, and a mime group, between 3 and 6 people.**

*Question and Answers are stage left, Question standing centrally behind Answers 1&2 who are seated either side of him. They address the audience, not each other. The mime group occupy stage right and centre stage. They respond to the statements made by the two Answers. You may wish one half of the mime group to respond to Answer 1 and the other to Answer 2, to differentiate between the two views held by each, or, especially if numbers are limited, everyone to respond to each Answer. The mime interpretations of the Answers should be simple and swift, just one movement and freeze until the next.*

**Question** What is man?

**Answer1** Man is the most intelligent and superior life-form.

**Answer2** Man is an animal.

**Q** What can man do?

**A1** Man can solve problems, theorise and philosophise.

**A2** Man can eat, sleep and reproduce.

**Q** What has man achieved?

**A1** Man has created a civilization, a complex social order.

**A2** Man sleeps inside at night and buys his food in Sainsbury's.

**Q** What has man made?

| | |
|---|---|
| **A1** | Man has made complex machinery to make life easier. |
| **A2** | Man has invented gas chambers and nuclear warheads. |
| **Q** | What has man done? |
| **A1** | Man has travelled into space, widened his boundaries. |
| **A2** | Man has spent billions on research while millions have starved. |
| **A1** | Man has found ways to develop and use the earth's resources to his own advantage. |
| **A2** | Man has begun to destroy his environment and the creatures he shares it with. |
| **A1** | Man has sought to resolve problems through reasoning and diplomacy. |
| **A2** | Man has succumbed to corruption and murder time after time and wages war on the innocent. |
| **Q** | What is man going to do? |
| **A1** | Man will advance, progress, become more intelligent, more powerful, he will rule the universe. |
| **A2** | Man will destroy all living creatures, himself, his planet. |
| | *(Pause and freeze for a moment.)* |
| **Q** | Man is created in God's own image, if only he could see his reflection. |
| | *(The following verses could then be spoken by the two Answers, or the whole cast could participate.)* |

Then God said,
"Let us make man in our image, in our likeness, and let them rule over the fish of the sea and the birds of the air, over the livestock, over all the earth, and

over all the creatures that move along the ground.

So God created man in his own image, in the image of God he created him; male and female he created them.

What is man that you are mindful of him, the son of man that you care for him? You made him a little lower than the heavenly beings and crowned him with glory and honour.

The Lord saw how great man's wickedness on the earth had become, and that every inclination of the thoughts of his heart was only evil all the time. The Lord was grieved that he had made man on the earth, and his heart was filled with pain.

And we, who with unveiled faces all reflect the Lord's glory, are being transformed into his likeness with ever-increasing glory, which comes from the Lord, who is the Spirit.

Put off your old self which is being corrupted by its deceitful desires... and put on the new self, created to be like God in true righteousness and holiness.

# The Smilers and the Miseries

*This was written for a primary school assembly to complement a general message about selfishness. The mime was performed by adults, but children would do it even better! Some schools are quite sensitive about overt evangelism, and this would perhaps be a good drama to start with if you're visiting a school for the first time and want to be invited back! Don't be afraid of performing it in front of older audiences as well. It could contribute to a family service, especially if it was performed by some of the children.*

**For narrator and group mime, at least 4.**

*No props are necessary, and I've not included any specific directions; the gaps in the story are where you can fit in movement and the story is specific enough for you to work out your own mime. Try to keep the story moving, but keep actions to a minimum during the narration to avoid distraction. You will need a minimum of 4 actors, in addition to the narrator. If you do perform this in a school you could encourage follow-up writing and drawing from the children, draw a smiler, a miserie, write a story about the miseries before they became smilers, etc etc...Even better, if you're a teacher, perform it with your class!*

Once upon a time there was a very happy land where the sun always shone.

The people who lived there were called the Smilers.

I think you can see why...

Their land was very beautiful with lots of parks and beaches for everyone to share.

The Smilers were always kind to each other and everyone was great friends.

They used to play together,

Look after each other,

And whatever they had, they shared.

If someone had some sweets, then everyone had one,

If someone was given a new toy, then everyone played with it,

No one was ever hungry, bored or lonely.

God loved to visit the Smilers, they always made him glad.

Then one day some visitors moved to the land.

They were called the Miseries.

The Smilers were very pleased to see them, everyone was welcome in their land.

But however much the Smilers smiled and laughed and looked after the Miseries, all the Miseries could do was frown and sulk.

The Smilers showed the Miseries their lovely land, but the Miseries dropped rubbish on the beaches and dug big holes in the parks so no one could play there.

The Smilers tried to play with the Miseries, but the Miseries spoilt the games by cheating so they always won.

If a Miserie got hurt the Smilers would try and look after them, but the Miseries would just hurt them as well.

When the Smilers shared their sweets with the Miseries, they just grabbed the whole packet and ate them all up.

When the Smilers let the Miseries play with their new toys, the Miseries either ran away with them, or broke them.

The Smilers were very confused. They'd never met miserable people before. They wished they could make them happy.

Then one day the Smilers woke up to find that the Miseries had put barbed wire round all their parks and beaches so they couldn't play on them any more.

The Smilers felt very miserable. They'd never felt miserable before.

And God was miserable too.

But the most miserable of all were the Miseries.

Even though they had the Smilers' land all to themselves they just weren't happy. They quarrelled and fought and stole from each other. In fact they became more miserable than ever.

Meanwhile the Smilers had to find somewhere else to play. One day they came across a grey rainy land with dirty beaches and parks full of broken toys. It was the land where the Miseries had come from.

The Smilers quickly got to work, helping each other to mend the toys and clean the beaches. They grew happier and happier as they worked together, and soon the sun began to shine. Before long the Miseries' land was just as beautiful as the Smilers' had been.

The sun had stopped shining on the Miseries though. One day, one of them was so fed up he decided to find out what the Smilers had been up to all this time.

When he saw how they had cared for the parks and beaches in his own land he felt very ashamed. He ran back and told all the other Miseries. They felt ashamed too, especially when they looked around them and saw what a mess they had made of the beautiful land the Smilers once had.

They decided to go and see the Smilers.

When the Smilers saw them coming they felt a little alarmed, but they greeted them just as warmly as they had before.

But the nicer the Smilers were, the more unhappy the Miseries became. They felt really dreadful.

At last one of them did something a Miserie had never done before. He offered a Smiler a sweet...

And as the Smiler took it with a surprised "Thank You!" the most wonderful thing happened. The Miserie smiled.

Then suddenly all the Miseries began sharing their sweets with the Smilers, and one by one they ALL began to smile!

Before they knew it, everyone was laughing and smiling and playing together in the sunshine.

And from that day on the Smilers and Miseries lived happily together. It did take a little while for the Miseries to learn not to be

**54**

selfish anymore, but the Smilers always helped them, and never called them the Miseries again.

And God was very, very glad, as he wants us all to live peacefully together, whether we're a Miserie, or a Smiler, or sometimes a bit of both!

# My Way

*This sketch was originally written for a school assembly, although it would suit any outreach situation. It went down very well in a pub recently and is a useful one to perform just before an evangelistic talk.*

**Characters Jude, Jim/Kim, Dot, Bold and Christian**

*There are five characters, and it is actually perfectly possible for just one person to perform all five, I know, I've done it in front of about 400 11-15 year olds! Props are essential in this case, and very slick changes, but just turning your back to the audience and having all props on a table behind you works quite adequately!*
*Jude wears trendy trainers, jeans, t-shirt, sunglasses and an earring (if female). Jim/Kim just removes the earring and sunglasses and adds a tennis racket. Dot puts on glasses and clutches a large ring binder. Bold puts a large Guns 'n' Roses (or similar) t-shirt over other clothes, and sticks a clip earring up one nostril. Christian removes t-shirt and earring and needs no props apart from sincerity! All the first four characters provide a splendid opportunity to overact! Although this sketch is written in the style of that ever popular song "My Way" no singing is required, but do say the words in the rhythm of the song, and by all means sing if you want to!*

**Jude**     My name is Jude, I'm a cool dude,
I wear the latest, trendiest fashions.
My shoes are mean, my hair is clean,
Shopping for new clothes is my greatest of passions.
I like to puff, and strut my stuff,
Down each and every single highway,
But more than this, much more than this,
I do things my way.

**Jim**
My name is Jim, I play to win,
'Cos I'm the best at every sport.
I shoot the goals, can vault with poles,
And every wicket by me is caught.
I like to swim, throw the javelin,
And in the Olympics one day I'll play.
But more than this, much more than this,
I do things my way.

**Dot**
My name is Dot, I am a swot,
I like to work hard at every lesson.
I'd like to be a brain surgeon maybe,
Or any other worthwhile profession.
I work each night, to get things right,
Do all my homework, and every single essay,
But more than this, much more than this,
I do things my way.

**Bold**
My name is Bold, I don't do as I'm told,
I'm what they call a bit of a rebel.
I like to shout, throw things about,
As for my language, my mum says it's terrible.
In loads of schools, I've broken all the rules,
Because I always must get my own say,
But more than this, much more than this,
I do things my way.

**Christian**
He died with our sin, for us to win,
Eternal life and peace forever.
Endured such pain, but rose again,
And now I know, He'll leave me never.
He gives to me, a life so free,
Unceasing love with every new day,
So as for me, yes as for me,
I'll do things His way.

# *Appendix One*

*Some tips for effective drama in evangelistic situations.*

**Context: The Evangelistic Church Service.**
**Possible sketches: The Interview, Off the Rails, Who am I?**

1.	Discuss with whoever is coordinating the whole service what the overall theme is likely to be. You may need to tailor your drama around this, or if you already have something in mind, give them a few ideas!

2.	Decide how many sketches it is feasible for you to rehearse in the given time schedule. It is better to have one brilliantly executed drama, than two or three mediocre ones.

3.	Decide where the best place in the programme will be for the sketch(es). One of my favourite formulas is a fairly mild, humorous one early on, even to break the ice at the start of the meeting, followed by a more serious, challenging one later, either just before, within, or even after the talk.

4.	If you do agree with the speaker to act close to, or in their talk, make sure they have a copy of the script well in advance, and if possible, that they actually come to a rehearsal to see the sketch performed.

5.	Make sure all the actors are aware of the running order of the meeting.

6.	Get together before the meeting begins, and rehearse in the space you have been allotted, especially if your rehearsals have previously been in someone's tiny sitting room!

7.	Think about how audible and visible you are likely to be to your audience/congregation. They will most likely all be seated. If you are too, only a few will see you. Given the acoustics, will you need a microphone?

8.      And most importantly, pray.

**Context: The Secondary School Assembly.**
**Possible sketches: What the RAM don't see..., My Way, What is Man.**

1.      Make sure that the school realises who and what you are. Most schools are only too happy to have someone offer to take an assembly, but they can be touchy about what you say and do. If you are at all unsure, go for a fairly mild assembly first, don't compromise on your message, but do remember, you want to be invited back!  We initially contacted several local schools a few years ago as part of an outreach week and we now have regular termly slots with most of them.

2.      Check the manpower you have available. If the majority of the drama group are at work between 9 and 3 on a weekday, are there students you can use or people with more flexible timetables? Most of our assemblies are performed by students and those of us who can take a few hours off work in the day.

3.      Make sure the assembly has a coherent theme that runs through everything you do. Your favourite sketch, followed by someone's favourite song, finished off with a favourite story may be entertaining but it's much better if they all link together! As you may be giving the first truly Christian assembly the pupils have ever seen, they need to be able to understand the message.

4.      A sketch is not enough. You will need someone to talk (briefly), and perhaps some Bible readings, a poem or two, a story, a performed song, someone to give their testimony etc. Of course, multi-talented as your drama group probably is, you may still need to import extra church members. The youth group leader is a good person to get hold of.

5.  Keep it concise. The school won't thank you if you run overtime. They have a timetable to keep to.

6.  Don't rely on having lots of props or a complicated set. You may not have the time or space to set them up. Your acting area may well be the two foot wide space between the closed stage curtain, and the 3 ft drop down to the hall floor.

7.  Don't patronise or talk down to the kids. Ask for the help of the teenagers in the church, they'll be very honest and tell you if they think there's anything you could change! You also want to be able to give the pupils who are already Christians a new opportunity to witness to their friends, not be embarrassed!

8.  Pray about it!

**Context: The Primary School Assembly.**
**Possible sketches: The Smilers and the Miseries, The Parable of the Rich Fool.**

1.  All the comments above for secondary assemblies are of course very relevant, with the exception of no. 6. In a way primary assemblies are more challenging because you will probably be addressing an audience from ages 4-11, which is an enormous span in understanding and conceptual development, far greater than that between the ages of 11 and 16 or 18.

2.  Get the children to join in. Teenagers are sometimes a bit too cool to sing, or do actions etc, but there's often no holding back younger children. Popular Christian childrens' songs, preferably with lots of actions, always go down wonderfully, even the real golden oldies like "Wide, wide as the ocean". Every school has a piano, or take a guitar (and someone who can play them!) You can also get the children to help you act, retell a story, answer questions etc.

3.  Your sketch should be simple to understand, as should

everything else. If you tell a story, use illustrations as well, drawn on a large board, or on OHPs.

4. Be kind to the teachers. Don't finish off with an all-dancing, shouting, jumping about song! By all means let them enjoy themselves but keep them calm at the end, before they go back to their classes. (The children that is!)

5. Expect to be invited back!

**Context: Street Outreach.**
**Possible sketches: In the Balance, The Astounding Jesus Rap, When You Wish Upon a Fairy.**

1. You really need one person who is prepared to co-ordinate the whole event.  Drama will probably be only one part of the things that happen. You will need singers, musicians, people willing to give a testimony or talk, possibly someone to do some sketch-boarding etc. Recruit as many people as you can to sing, hand out tracts, help form an audience when you act, and generally be available to talk to people.

2. Check the legalities of free performing in your area. It may be wise to notify the police. (In Cambridge you are permitted to use a public address system if it is a 'religious service' but city and town regulations differ.)

3. An overall theme isn't really necessary as your audience will be coming and going and only seeing part of the action. Your aim is to get their attention for as long as possible, and once you've got it, to keep it.  A noisy, exciting drama will often pull a large crowd in a way that nothing else will.

4. Wear costumes, even if it's only jeans and coloured T-shirts. This will make it easier for the crowd to spot you and work out who's acting and who's a bystander.

5. If you can, use a microphone, or be prepared to speak very loudly! Practise in a large back garden and send someone to the other end to try and hear you.

6.	Find a good pitch. This may take several tries. A central area in a precinct is good, or any pedestrianised area where there is a good steady flow of human traffic. Try not to poach other people's areas. In a city like Cambridge where there are many buskers you sometimes have to come to an agreement with those around you, especially if they're a rock band!

7.	Find somewhere central to congregate, pray together, and rehearse before you go. We use a nearby house, or a city centre church.

8.	Be prepared for hecklers. If possible ignore them, or have someone designated to deal with them, who can draw them away and talk to them quietly somewhere else!

9.	Mix up your programme, songs, drama, testimony, songs, talk, drama etc. Keep the ball rolling. A testimony or talk is often good after a drama as you can catch a large captive audience! Experiment with just single sketches, or two or three put together.

10.	Enjoy it! Street theatre often seems more terrifying than it really is. Remember Ezekiel when you're out there! He did it first!

# *Appendix 2*

The song 'Interface' from the cassette 'One to One' by Geoff Twigg is available from Bodyworks, 7 Pound Road, Bury, Huntingdon, Cambs, PE17 1LB. Contact Bodyworks at the above address if you wish to use the song.

Below are some rough plans for the balance scales for 'In the Balance', with suggestions for weights for the bricks.

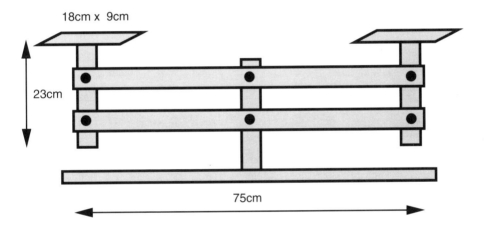

The cross pieces and verticals were made of planed 2" x 1" (actually 44mm x 19mm) pine wood. The base was made from a plank of wood and the platforms were made of thick plywood. The wood was drilled and movement was enabled with long bolts, washers and self-locking nuts.

The bricks were made of plywood with dimensions 6" x 4" x 2" (15cm x 10cm x 5cm) and painted. The weight of the bricks was increased where necessary by filling with nails.

5 White bricks:  approx  250g each
5 Black bricks:  4 of these weighed 250g and the other one weighed about 3kg
1 Red brick:      approx 5kg

A final plea for help.

In addition to the sketches in this book, there are many others that we as a group perform that I would have loved to include in this book. Most of them have been handed down from friend to friend from all over the country with no idea of the original author. I'd like to include them in Act Two, so if anyone knows where the copyright rests for 'Little Billy and Big Joe', 'The Race', 'Hands', 'D'ja Wanna Be a Rebel', 'Wet Paint' or that special celebrity 'Reginald Melling' (complete with bananas), please contact me via Coastline Christian Resources. If nothing else, I can at last ask for permission to perform them!